My Heart is Non-Binary.

By: AJ Smith.

ISBN. 978 0 359 06184 6

Welcome to my Non-Binary world!

Hello! My name is AJ Smith.

I was born on August 4th 1992. the way everyone
else was born, except I was different
I knew it from the moment when I could choose
how to dress myself and choose what toys I was
going to play with.
It was at that young carefree age that I knew
something wasn't right.
Like my body just didn't agree with what was in
my mind.
like some sort of sick mind game that only you
can figure out.
I chose to transition into a male, as I was born
a female and knew that wasn't who I was.
Not knowing at the time what a non-binary person
was or even what non-binary even meant, I went
ahead and started on testosterone for two whole
years. I knew who I was at that time, until one
day I just decided that wasn't the life I wanted
to live anymore. So I took the biggest step in
my life and chose to stop testosterone and my
transition.
Not because I didn't feel that I was a male but
because I felt that I needed to truly find out
who I was before I could push forward. It's been
almost 6 years since I stopped living life as a
male and I have no regrets because I'm still
learning and growing into the person I need to
be.

Most of my childhood years I had to fight for my
life.

I lived with my drug addicted mother and an apathetic father that never cared to do anything about it… well until this year where after 26 years of dealing with my mom, my dad choose to leave the abuse and start anew.
I'm proud of him for that, but now at 26 years old, I now have the responsibility to look after him. He's 82 and has nothing more than myself and my loving partner to make sure he's okay.
I call that learning to forgive the past as much as it hurts. My life has been full of moments of sadness, but I won't let my childhood anger take over and not let me help my old dad.

Okay…
Let's rewind a bit so you all can kinda get where this book is coming from and the content behind it.
If at any point you are confused about my poems or any of my writing feel free to message me on my social media with any and all questions you may come up with.
I'm going to make this kinda short but sweet, so hold on to your socks everyone.
I was kicked out at 15 because my mother chose to beat the shit out of me (excuse my language) and unfortunately that wasn't the last time she would try to hurt me, but she had told me I was no longer welcome in the home.
It was at that time in my life where I was just trying to figure out what kind of human I wanted to be in this world.
what I wanted to do with my life type deal.

I had nothing but the clothes on my back and
this constant will to keep pushing on.
Through everything I ever went through,
I knew for myself that I was stronger braver
then most.
I knew that someday someone would look at me
and see the whole world in my eyes,
The way I look at the world is simple:

Be a good human. You never know who you might
impact in your life. Make the most of the life
you have and don't ever let your traumas or your
demons control your life. Live it and just be
you.
That's all that anyone can do.

Now without further ado.
I bring to you a collection of my poems written
in every stage of my life so far.

Struggling?
It's okay I am too
These words you are about to read is my darkness
And light
Through and through
These words are knowing new
More so lessons and reasons
Of starting anew
A new being this book
Which now belongs to you.

-Take care of you

CONTENTS:

My heart is Non-Binary is split into sections on:

Feel free to pick a spot or read from page 1.

ACKNOWLEDGMENTS:

This book is dedicated to Camille:
The love that was found at a very broken time in my life. Everything happens for a reason and she's my reason. I hope you enjoy reading my book as much as I enjoyed writing about you.
I love you so much.

This book is also dedicated to my client:
You have brought so much joy into my life and really has cheered me on this crazy journey. Thank you for helping me push through life, while helping you be the best you.

To Laura:
This lady has really been a second mom to me and has taken me in at Christmas time when I had no one and nowhere to go, Christmas will always be a time where I reflect on how people actually cared about me. Thank you for showing me a family love I never really had.
I love you and the family.

And to everyone else who has from day one rooted for me and the making of this book.
Thank you all.

One:

LOVE...

You're the only one I need
the only one for me
my heart tells me so
but I'm a mess baby
please forgive me.

-forgive the mess

Love is something that profound's your soul
leaving nothing but
the will to keep being strong
If not for her but for you.

-I got it, it's easy.

When you choose to love someone with demons
You choose to live with them,
just like you live with yours.

-My demons are yours now.

I promise with my whole heart
That every time you feel broken
Or life is too hard to bare
I'll kiss your pain away always.

Love and life really is
a consistent battle
to be yourself and to love yourself
So at the end of the day
and you just want to wash all the pain
you pushed and took with you all day,
just remember that you matter
you're beautiful and
the first step to life is
not loving her first
but loving you first.

Broken and bare
with nothing there
I found love
love that touches
your spine and
gives you those little hairs
that stick way up
every time
you touch me
and for once
it feels right.

I love women
who doesn't?
but when I met you
I never wanted a woman
ever again
I was done
I was broken and blue
I couldn't
I wouldn't
ever date another woman

-Until I found you

Your lips and your hips
is what pulled me into your world
and now your world is my world
and I don't want anyone else's world
in my world besides yours.

I was born into a family
who doesn't know the word love
or how one must love
love meant hate
and hate is what pushed me into the life
I live now
family isn't everything
and I hope one day my family learns to love
like I've learned to love myself.

Picture this:
cute tinder date
you decide to meet
and to go up to her apartment
you have to take an elevator up and it's packed
you're nervous, and smashed up against that
cute tinder date
Yes that did indeed happen
and yes I am completely in love with that cute
tinder girl
who stole my heart
and maybe even my soul when we squeezed
together
on that very packed elevator.

Walking down the hall
I stop after I see you running tracks around
the gym
you stop and smile
I smiled and walked away
but what you don't know is that smile
never really went away.

I'm at the gay bar
I look around check out the crowd
I turn and see you
I see you in the corner
dancing by yourself with no care
in the world
she was wearing pearls and
a black short wig and
was more out then you could ever be
that's the person who I seen
because I spend my time looking at the misfits
and the unseen
that person looking at her was me
and I think you're beautiful, to me.

You've got a way of getting into my mind
you know me better then I even know myself
you take me in as is
and you love me
and not the love that you always see in movies
but you truly love me
even when I have no more motivation to carry on
even when the darkness intrudes my soul.

I'm never going to be easy to love.
we're on survivors land every day
everything that's good
we can write in the sand
but baby
If only you promise not to let go of my hand.

I'm a mess
this is quite true
but every time I come home to you
you ease the mess
you love when loving me
was all that you wanted it to be.

I'm
so in love
with you.
your face is
pretty
neat too.

Love means no harm
if there is harm there is no love
don't settle for the love you think you deserve
love has no weekends
love doesn't take breaks
so when you're weak
do not settle for that last beat
you know it's not going to be the last time
they hit you
even if they say they love you.

She's in a wheelchair yes.
does she feel or see when you're staring at her
making her undoubtedly uncomfortable?
Yes.
Because she can't talk doesn't mean
she can't hear or see
the faces you make at her in
disability disbelief

-Be kind to every single person you meet

You have all the things I need.
all the things that reside in my mind
that I know to be love.
you show my crazy how to be
and how to see that all you have to do
is love me and everything will just be.

-That's the story of you and me

Love is all you need
but it's not everything
please don't tell yourself
that you need someone
because that makes you feel whole
fuck that shit
Be you
nothing is whole until the moment when
you learn to love
every minute of every second
of your soul.

-Love yourself first.

Teach me how to love and nothing more
bring me peace to my core
tell me I'm beautiful
and that you care about me
but don't you ever lay a finger on me.

These moments
these tiny little moments
I spend with you in bed
makes me forget about why
I was ever that sad.

My fingers run down her body so softly
that she giggles and begs me to stop
but I can't stop
she is the most beautiful woman
I have ever seen
then she turns to me
and whispers guess what?
You're in me
my body leans into her
and in this moment
she is all the world needs.

We both struggle
we knew this when we chose
to love each other
I know this will be hard
and maybe at times
to put it lightly
A mother fucker
but just know
I'm always going to love her.

It may take months
maybe years
to fall in love with yourself
so once you're done reading this book
put me on the shelf and
go learn to love and honour yourself.

Baby if you fall and you can't get back up
I'll start a war
I'll push till the end of days
to prove to you that I'm worthy of you
cause baby if I make you fall and
you can't get up, I'd start a war
and blame it all on myself
because I'm nothing else
without you
and it's true
because every day my mind starts a riot
and you always hold me
till everything feels just quiet.

Girlfriend-ship:
the essence of learning
to love yourself and be a best friend
to your spouse.

I hold my breath so you don't need to
yet you're the only one
who feels the way I do
you clean up the mess
sweep away the distress
and at the end of the day we still sit down
and talk
even when you don't have to
but you need to
and see that is the only person for me.

I love you more than my internal self
like more than this book that soon will be on
our shelf
knowing that I wrote this for you
dedicated to you and my true few
so when this book is no longer new
please give it to someone that's struggling
like you too.

I have baggage
but you're the only thing
that's keeping me awake at night
cause I roll over and
I'm caught in your sweet dreams
holding me with your tight embrace
and oh so cute face.

I will live paycheck to paycheck
for the rest of my life
as long as you'll be my wife.

She took me by surprise
came into my life
when I was nothing but cold
now she knows how to
turn this black heart warm again
just by the way she looks at me.

Little fights, tiny fights
about fake sugar
is nothing because
we can't even go 60 seconds
without kissing, forget the sugar!
Baby just let me take your face
and kiss your sweet lips.

One time I "tried"
to have a food fight
in our own kitchen
in the middle of the night
when everyone was sleeping
Camille didn't like it much
and that was truly the only time
I've ever seen the love of my life
mad at me with zucchini pancakes
in her hair
I fell in love with her all over again
even if she still smelt like garlic
I didn't care.

February 25, 2018.

It was a cold February night
when we decided to be a thing
we held each other in bed
with no worries
but the demons we had in our head
I asked you to be my girlfriend
and you cried, holding me oh so tight
I remember that night because
baby all of our memories are so new
I don't even know how someone like you
could love someone like me
with all the broken pieces
but you do.

I knew it was you
It had always been you
To fall for me is to fall for
The fights
The tears
The fears
the up at all hours of the night
The I need space
and most importantly you love me
even when my past lover hurt me
She took everything I knew about me
She really did hurt me
And yet you still take your time
Every single day
To love me.
For all of me.
That's when I knew
I was going to be forever falling for you.

Truth be told
true love does indeed find you
I was not looking
when I took that very daring fall
and risked it all for you.

My heart beats really fast
when you look into my eyes
I'm sure you'll see my past
but please don't look at that.

I've told you many times you could leave
pack your bags and be done
but you chose to stay with what is
and you chose to love me
even though I'm not a great person
You took me in
you showed me that love is real
and in this moment
while you lay half naked in our bed
I know that even the things
that are left unsaid
you still love and support me
even if I'm sick in the head.

I want fall to be here already
I want to crunch the leaves with my feet
try and find good vegan Halloween treats
sweaters that are too tight
but it's alright
cause it's so cute on you
chilly fall nights
pumpkin spice everything
and I want you in my arms
every single cold night.

I want to love you for the rest of my gays.

TWO

DARKNESS...

Trigger warnings

the warning before the storm
some people choose to read warnings
and quotations telling you STOP!
It's best unseen
But yet you still uncover and read them
and watch as storms form
and nothing is left
but broken lies
that can't be unseen.

4 years of my life was spent trying to preform
for you
like a clown
I performed for you
tried to make you laugh
tried to make you happy
with what was the existence of us
but nothing of that mattered to you
you left me helpless
and when I needed you the most
you were nothing but a flying balloon
in the sky.

Home is a place where you call home
where you sleep at night
where everything feels right.
my phone is where I call life
where life isn't pain
and pain isn't feeling
it's where I can feel unknown.

-Caller unknown.

I remember
the first time you pushed me
to the floor
like a chip that falls out of the bag
when you're watching your favourite show
like Netflix without the chill
falling into the air and onto my knees
the harder you pushed
the more I stayed and I stayed for 2 more years
after that.

-I will never look at chips the same.

Dear Dad:

Mom beat you like she beat me
she took advantage of you
and hurt your soul
You turned to me when you had nothing left
and we're alone
but I had nothing left
I didn't know how to support you
when for the past 10 years
you weren't there
my life was always without you
so I built up my walls that I worked so hard on
...again
so that I can be there for you because you're
82.

Love: AJ

Dear Mom:

I am grateful for you bringing me
into this world
but that is all I'm here to say
because you took everything else
I knew when I was little away
and I hope one day you will understand
the pain you put me through
but this letter I will never send
because you would burn that too.

I tried to kill myself
5 times
that's 5 moments
of unwanted feelings
of loneliness, depression
and most of all darkness
I'm a survivor and human
so are you
Never
Give
Up.

Take me for my demons
let them work their way into your heart
know that my demons want nothing more
then to be in your blood stream
and then when your demons hurt you
blood is shed, wounds open
and nothing is left but my demons
and that's where they will call home
that's when they will heal your demons.

-Home is where your demons are

The drugs had nothing on me
I let you be mom
you see while you pretended to play mom
I learned just what kind of human you were
the drugs had nothing on me
I let you be.

I lost you not once, not twice
not even three times
I lost you the whole 7 years
we were friends
I tried to find you
but you got lost
trying to find me.

-7 years gone

This day and age we rely on likes
double taps on Instagram
comments of emoji's
but no real words or emotions attached
we all know what it's like
posting a photo
getting a like
I'd lie and say I don't do it for the likes
but I do.

-Far too many likes

11:24pm:

It's not that I miss you
it's not that I want to even think about you
it's the way I long to know if you're okay
even though you wouldn't ask
to see how am doing.

Lightning in the storm
baby you're the storm
when it rains it pours
baby am the lightning
when it strikes it burns.

Life gets too hard to bare sometimes
people try to find ways to hid the pain
like drinking and doing drugs
so the next time you blame
your alcoholic father
or your drug ridden mother
think and ask yourself is it wrong to feel
nothing at all?
my answer is no.

Let me wash away the demons
like they were never born in your mind
let me wipe away the tears
that keep you up at night
come with me, I want to show you the light
and if the light doesn't come
let's just sit in the dark together
because tomorrow is a new night
and at some point soon there will be light.

If you only knew
my dad is 82
my mom used to put locks on the fridge
and the cupboards
so that my dad couldn't make food
or do anything in the house he called home
that is the kind of environmental abuse
that I was put through too.

Have you ever been in love
with a broken heart?
at least one of you in this life time
will in fact experience
the gut wrenching heartache
of being in love
while still grieving the heart brokenness
of your last relationship
but maybe you haven't experienced that and
that's okay too
because we are all human
with our own stories
and our own beautiful
but sometimes crazy minds.

Touch me
tell me that everything will be okay
and maybe just for one night
it will be
touch me softly
before it all gets lost
and you see nothing
but the touches of how
we used to be.

I'm under water
my feet feel like rocks
maybe there really in my socks
pulling me down
and until one day I do drown.

Exhausted and tired
yet you smile
because it's what we are made to do
in this society
we are made to fake these smiles
and pretend that nothing hurts
but in the end the only thing
we have left
is the fake shit and smiles
that keep appearing
will there ever be an end?

Where were you mom when I needed you
it's so hard without you
but you never needed me
like I needed you
hey dad now that your 82
and you didn't need me when I was 15
just like I needed mom
or when you needed to need me
but you couldn't bare too
but now I still sit here wondering
why am I helping you
when you never thought to help me
when I needed you to need me too.

Crying is like swimming
when you're under water you can't breathe
just like at night when you're at home alone
crying.

-It's like swimming really

When they were young
they knew they were dumb
learning at a slow pace is all they ever knew
fast forward to age 25
And life still makes them slow.

-they weren't always slow.

10 years of not having you in my life:

How could you kick me out mom?
I have nowhere to go.
Age 15.

Where were you when I needed you?
I miss you.
Age 16.

This will be the last time you ever touch me.
Age 17.

You are nothing but a fucked up mess,
why are you still on drugs?
Age 18.

I learned everything without you, where were you
for this life heart break?
I'm so broken.
Age 19.

I'm in love mom and I went to college, where the
fuck are you?
right you're with the drugs.
Age 20.

Why won't you call me? Why won't you wish me
happy birthday?
Age 21.

I'm done caring about you.
Age 22.

....
Age 23.

....
Age 24.

I saw you again. Thank goodness you didn't see
me on the bus, you were looking unhappy as
normal. Are you happy with the life you gave me?
I heard you talking about me,
you said I was 26.
You are wrong.
Age 25.

Months have gone by
the love is gone
the feelings of loneliness have disappeared
but yet I still think of you once a month.

-It's been months.

Your love was toxic
like an oil spill killing thousands to millions
of living beings in the ocean
swimming for their life
hoping not to lose their friends
because you decided to put your toxic oil in my
ocean.

I loved you for 4 whole years
I gave you everything I could
you saw my mental health
you knew I struggled with everyday life
you knew I wanted to make you my wife
or I couldn't or really wouldn't have
asked you to be anything less
of what you gave me
which was nothing
but yet I'm still broken
and in love with another
and I still can't get over you
but that's the cycle of abuse.

I was 15, you were 28
it wasn't right
you knew better
but you did it anyway
and that's what happened
on that very rainy day
in the back of that car.

You don't know me
you only know what you heard online
or from someone who grew cold towards me
told you
yet you judge me
but you still don't know me.

If love is what you're after
don't look for it here
Tears. Tears. Tears.
run down their face
hopeless nothingness inside
but trying not to look like a disgrace.

I got down on one knee
asked her will you marry me?
still on my knee
feeling the cool December air
she looks and says that's it
like I wasn't there
why did I ever get down on one knee
if that was the way you treated me.

Medical Cannabis helps me with unwanted urges of
slitting my wrist.
Medical Cannabis helps me get out of bed when
staying in the dark is hard to resist.
Medical Cannabis is not for everyone so please
don't insist I quit.
Medical Cannabis helps me count the reasons to
stay alive instead of letting go of the will to
try.

Bed time is the only time
where I can get away from
the restlessness of having to be an adult
or a professional
on the daily
I just wish when I lay my head down at bed time
that someone would come pick me up and save
me.

they're crazy, maybe
but look beyond the fact
that they're crazy
beyond the tears and the madness
is someone who just wants to feel you
they're crazy for you
and in life they're crazy because of what they
went through
they're breaking
and all they need is you.

I broke you
you looked at me in the eyes
and told me all you had to say
goodbye is all I see
but baby please don't leave
I know I broke you
but I never ever meant to hurt you

I'm hard to handle
I have no filter
I always keep it real and raw
sometimes my filter gets me in trouble
I've lost friends, memories and
most importantly I lost me.

Please tell me it's okay
and that you're okay
because baby
I'm not going to let the darkness
surround you, even if it's made by me.

Broken from the abuse
I refuse to give myself this noose.

She dropped to the floor and cried
because you decided to send flirty messages to
the boy you had on the side
She cried
because she trusted you
she never wanted to hurt you
she wanted everything with you
but you were to busy to remember
because all you wanted
was something about you.

It's almost been 7 months
when we decided to stop being friends
your call this time, like every other single
time
I'm sorry I knew better
yet I treated you like the weather these days
dark and gloomy
but you knew me
you knew I was hard to deal with
hell you knew what I've been through too
this isn't the last time I think of you
But I'm so glad you wrote me on Instagram to
tell me
Happy Birthday.
Even if that's all you want to say
I'll take it
and walk away
like you did on that gloomy
February day.

You can rip my heart out all you want
the demons always stay
even if you get down on your knees
and pray.

One second you're in love
not thinking or knowing
what you're made of
wishing kisses were enough
but it's not enough you see
because all you had to do
was tell me I broke you
I really broke you
I hope one day you can forgive me
for all the things I've put you though.
I didn't mean to hurt you.

Genderless
sick in the head mess
broken and happy with all the stress disabled
non the less.
call it whatever you want
but what's it to you?

You see my client relies on me
to make sure her needs are met
but what happens when I need me?

Screams and tears
it's what I fear, it's all I hear
I fear that one day
the screams will stay
and the tears will fill our pillows
like it's nothing new
all because I did this to you.

These nights are the nights
that I wish I could fast forward through
you see last year I got out of a pretty bad
relationship
ever since I've been writing about it
through the hard times and the good
and these are the nights when
I get so much writing done
when my mind is going crazy
I hope one day you'll pick up my book
and say hey, this book actually saved me.

I used to wait for you
till you got home
because you thought it was best
that you took a night shift job
without talking about it with me first
you know to see if I was okay with
always sleeping alone and without you
most nights id stay up
and watch Shaw pay per view
just so I could see you and make sure you were
alright
when you got home
but all those nights
I wanted more, I needed you
did you need me?
until one night where I chose to leave
because this just wasn't right
it wasn't just the sleepless nights alone that
got me
it was the fact that when you got home in the
morning
you would get mad at me
because you had a bad night or you were cranky
sorry but you were never the one who was going
to save me.

Three:

HOLDING ON...

Hold on a little longer now
there is no time to give in
no time to give up
you're beautiful and don't let anyone fool you
you're strong when being strong
is all you ever had.

-Just hold on a little bit longer.

Leaving and learning to leave
is something that is completely different
leaving is easy but with you
I had to learn to leave, nothing else I could
do.

-Life is about learning

You're a drug
and someday you'll realize
that I'm not going to get over
this addiction
you have all I want
and my soul has risen.

Adult living is living
when you don't know how you can live like an
adult
but you wake up every day with hope in your
soul
and love in your eyes.

Adult living is seeing your friend
working at the grocery store
once a week and all you can do is say hi
just a "hey how are you doing"
kind of question and then you walk away
nothing is like it used to be.

-So be the best adult you wish to see.

Being in bed with you
is something I knew I needed
from the first day we decided to meet
and you took me into your room
showed me your med shelf
that is the day
I knew that I wasn't just
going to have to be strong for myself.

It's been months
yes I still think about you
the way you treated me
the way everything was about you and nothing
was about me
I'm stronger, wiser now.
So here's to you boo
Fuck you.

My heart is at its max
let me climax all the dreams
we have of you and me
just like you let me stay,
after I was the one who broke you
and you chose not to walk away.

Be wild, be true
and most importantly in this life
be fucking you.

People will always tell you
what you want to hear
even if it's not true
It's like they know when it's time to share
something you want to hear
but to me if it's not true
please don't repeat.

She's in pain
you have to support her
listen to her when she's had a bad day
sometimes just a caring word
is all you have to say
to let her know that she's okay.

Beaten and abused
life has always got in the way
kicked out at 15
helpless
with nothing but the thoughts of thinking
I can't make it out alive
I'm 25 now and I'm still alive.

I'm useless for trying
to make you feel better
but just know that this feeling
that you're feeling won't last forever.

Co-worker: Burned out? Ha you're okay! Just get over it. Do your job and go home, it's all about the pay!

Me: Working in health care was never about the pay for me
or it won't ever be easy
see the burn out is real
and most days I can't take care of myself
it hurts to feel
but I get up and do it
not for me but for my client
who at this moment needs me, like I need me.

-Take care of yourself health care professionals.

Calgary born and raised
some people call this home
but I call it Rome
cause one day
I'll ROME the FUCK out of here.

You have so much for this world
so much to give and so much to forget.

It's actually been really hard on my end
but obviously a lot of queer and non-queer
people know
what it's like to struggle with something or
another
my girlfriend and I both struggle with the same
mental disorder and it's actually so hard
because every time I look at her
all I see is me wanting to get better
so that I can love her and help her get better
you know, like the way normal people do.

I was 5 and young
that's when you stopped being my mom
it's been 10 years and I forgive you
forgive you for all the bad
you put me through
cause I'm better than that
better then you.

I fill my coffee cup on Sunday mornings
with this instant coffee
that makes adulthood seem more real
yet Sunday's is the only day
where I choose not to feel.

July 30th 11:13pm.

Pain is what I feel I can't hide what is real
within the deep dark dreams of my life
my purpose for this book
is not to only help others
who at some point will go through something
and they will feel like they're alone and that
there is no hope
I want young readers or elders alike
to know that life indeed goes on
and the pain that you feel is truly real
and you are valid.

Be you
if nothing else in the world
be that person you always wanted
to see in this world
but you didn't know how to get there
it all starts with you.

Past: I liked that you wanted to read your books
beside me, but were you hiding some sort of pain
or just not wanting to feel insane?

I know what you were trying to do
that's why I had to put an end to you.

Future: I know your weakness
I know you're pain
please take my hand because
you and I are the same
you get me and the friends
that we do have together
think were lame
but future don't worry because I'll take all
the blame.

-The past is not new, I'm in love with the
future which is you.

Messy places, Constantine faces
no matter where you go
yes you will see other races
be kind don't step out of line
they are human
let them shine.

Tuesday is the day I chose to stay
not because life or
no matter how hard you cried got in the way
I chose to stay
and from this point on I'm staying
you stay too because you matter
next Tuesday will be better.

-It was a Tuesday

I'm holding out my hands in the air
touching the rain
holding it because feeling wetness between my
palms
is what I needed to stay
and right now the world needs to know that I'm
here
I'm queer
and I know what it feels like to be used and
broken
I'm here to say that it's okay to cry
stand your ground
never back down
because once you back down is the day
you put down your crown.

There's a difference between
being sad and having depression
being sad sometimes only last a day or two
but with depression
it makes it hard to push through
day after day
It's okay to be sad too.

-Hang in there beautiful human

Aug 2, 2018
It's my birthday on Saturday I'll be 26
and for the first time
I really don't care to celebrate
it's really just a reminder
that you're getting old
like give me a break.

If you want something
go for it
you might end up regretting it
when you're 82
with nothing left in life but the wrinkles
that hide the pain
with knowing you didn't do
what your heart intended to.

I can't sleep tonight because
that blinking blinker light
telling my mind which way to go
won't let me sleep
until my mind is at home.

My heart is broken
but my soul knows what it's meant to do
don't stop believing in you!

Take my hand
let's walk through the sand
even when it's too hard to keep a float
I will always be here
with my rescue boat.

Crying and blowing your nose on shirts
is what really goes on
when you're an adult
and when you want to stop crying
and move on
but you're left with this silly nightie on
with your face and shirt filled with snot
and just for once you want to
slow down the pace
untie this crazy life knot
one day the nights of snots will stop
and you will learn to push through the
thoughts.

fuck live, laugh, love
and all of that
don't follow those
sappy quotes
find something that you can relate to
that you can feel
that makes life more real.

Do not listen to what others say about you
Unless they know you, all of you
like
how you couldn't go to bed without a goodnight
kiss
but no one was there to send you off to
dreamland bliss
like a rocking chair with no rock but it
persists
all you have is mismatched socks and you're so
okay with that
how you go to work and
you actually put effort into it
don't ever put down that motivation
to live through the dark and cold weather
live on and hopefully one day you will feel a
whole lot better.

I did it!
I made it to year 26
and really it feels like bliss
from leaving an abusive ex
crazy amounts of regrets
learning to love myself
and my gender identity
meeting the woman of my dreams
and she's all I need to succeed
Year 26 you be good to me.

Take care of your body
take care of your soul
but don't ever let your mind
be in control.

You're strong
I know you are
put down that phone
and go for a walk
grab Starbucks
enjoy the world
and most importantly
enjoy being you
without social media
it's not helping you recover
it's helping you slumber
and you don't need that, do you?

-Your phone doesn't control you

I'm so happy without you
you'll know when to run
but don't spend your whole life
looking at the sun
cause it will burn
the moon knows what to do
just be strong, hold on
and you'll know there is more than this
for you.

My poems are dark, sad and happy
but just know that
my writing is my real life
the world now knows
just goes to show
that people are indeed
stronger then you know

Hanging out with friends is nothing new
it's something in this society
tells us we need to do
to live a healthy lifestyle, I agree fully
but DON'T choose friends
who can't take you for your darkness
you need friends who understand
every single part of you
That's the kind of friends
I knew I needed
when the friends that knew me
chose to throw me away.

-Just choose wisely

Sometimes you have to take a break
a break from life or work
or even from your partner
it's okay to do these things
never feel like you have to partake.

I promised myself the next time
I ask another woman to marry me
it will be someone who treats me
with the utmost respect and dignity.

November 11, 2017

was the last breath you took out of me
I left you
I got the courage
and I really left you
after years of abuse
I'm so glad that my worth
is put to better use now
that you aren't around
putting my whole self-down
It took everything out of me to leave
but you see I have better now
and there is so much release
to know that I'm not with you anymore
you fragmented beast.

You know what I miss most about childhood?
swinging on the swings high in the air
with nothing but memories of childhood
that I choose not to share.

Life is like an amusement park ride
you're excited about the ride
you sit and wait
the ride takes off
and you knew you had made a mistake
by choosing that ride
but you go on it anyways
and you ride, ride, ride
until life isn't fun anymore
and you want to get off
you loosen the handles
and you thank yourself
that you're still alive.

-The story of how an amusement park ride saved
my life.

I want to kiss away my pain on your lips
hold me close don't let me go
cause I don't want to miss this
as I go into your sweet lips
thinking man for once this is how it feels
to not feel dismissed.

Life is rocky and it's hard to bare
half the time I don't even care
deodorant? Fuck it
hairs a mess? that's me I guess
but you know what matters the most?
is that I'm still here standing
alive in this world
I made it another day
don't listen to what your mind has to say
just take it with stride
and know that everything
will soon be alright
even if the light only stays bright
for a few more nights
hold on and don't ever think you're not strong.

I know it's hard to do
but get up and be you.
drive/take a walk to the mailbox
grab coffee
go to the mall to window shop
(If you can handle window shopping that is)
get together with friends even if you feel
uneasy about it you'll regret if you don't
fuck yes go on tinder/plenty of fish
just be safe
and maybe you'll find someone who could be a
new chapter
in your life I know I did
whatever you do
Please don't just sit there
in dark and in silence
there is more to this world that you need to see
and you need to be alive to see it all
I believe in you.

We fall for each other fast
we both know this is true
but every time I look at you
I know I've made the right decision
you make me a whole new person
you know my weakness
you know how to make me hot
and with that I'm going to love you
until there is no more of you to love.

It takes courage to look in the mirror
and tell yourself that you're beautiful
but you know and I know that you're a beautiful
human.

Flesh and bone
all I need is warm oxygen to breathe.

Tell me I don't keep you up a night
tell me that you don't think about me
with the thoughts of day dreams is all we were
meant to be
just trust baby because you know I'm not
crazy.

I can't stop thinking about it
it's on mind
The act of being able to be free,
set me free, let me be me
but I can't do that you see
because that would be wrong.

-Cheating is never the answer.

My demons have found home in you
and I don't know what to do.

Four

GENDER IDENTITY.

(My story of non-binary)

My weight is all on my chest
these breasts are no longer welcome here.

Are you a boy or a girl?
all my life was always mess of
what are you?
Do you have a penis?
Do you have both?
Why do you have a deep voice
but you look like a girl?
my response now is that
"does it matter to you?"
Or really does my gender expression
really matter to you?
why go out of your way
to ask someone if they are
a gender?
so to answer your questions
about my individual identity
as a human race
I am me
Sorry if that wasn't what you wanted to hear.

143.

Stop it, stop with the gender pronouns
can't we just live in a world
where we don't have to live with what people
see
on the outside?
and just live freely being whoever the fuck you
want?

Sometimes I'm a girl and sometimes I'm a boy,
sometimes I hide both in the closet
because I like just feeling free to be me.

My hope for the future
is that people who struggle
with any form of gender dysphoria
know that regardless of how they feel
or how they think they should feel
or be for social media
and really the world
that it's okay, just be you
I know it's hard
I've been there too
just stand up and tell them
that you're you and that's more than enough
to shape your view
and what others think of you
be in this moment
and love who you are
even when gender
is still so black and blue.

```
                 Gender?
              what's this?
                That's it
                 fuck it
         just call me genderless.
```

You look at me and see boy
a boy with long hair
but there's more to me then that
your stares lasting longer and longer
until one day
I looked in the mirror and
said to myself
that I'm not going to ever
let myself live in fear.

I want to run in the sun
with a field full of flowers
like the ones you see
on those really popular Instagram's
running through sunflowers of time
running in a dress
but then when I get to the end
I see me in a suit
looking oh so handsome and cute
then I run to you
and you still love me
even in a dress and or a suit.

I was in elementary in grade 3 or 2
went to the girls bathroom
when a girl comes in and screams
there's a boy in here!
she runs out and comes back with a teacher
that was the first time
that my mind agreed with me
I was a boy inside all along
standing in that bathroom
little me was happy even
if it was only for a second

-To the girl who got the teacher: Thank you!

Yes I AJ Smith,
detransitioned
it's true
I didn't think it though
It wasn't something that I wanted to do.
(detransition that is)
but the truth is
I'm still growing
I have so much more growth to do
before I fly away.
but for now call me Non-Binary.

You're alive
it's just up from here
keep holding on
you're worthy of life
you're a magical human
if I have to stay
you have to, too

ABOUT THE AUTHOR:

AJ is a non-binary, indigenous
and androgynous poet
who has opened up their life to everyone on
social media.
To bring awareness on mental health and gender
identity with no filter.
AJ lives life often on heartfelt conversations
and truth.
AJ shares life and living with gender identity
issues when most people are unable to share.
Life is about meaning and
My Heart Is Non-Binary is here to show you that
it's okay to just live your true self
that you're valid and you are definitely not
alone.

If you're interested in following their journey
of life on Instagram follow:
Ajaysworld242

Lightning Source UK Ltd.
Milton Keynes UK
UKHW040921020719

345421UK00001B/51/P

9 780359 061846